Written by Bec and Max Smith.
Illustrated by David Robinson.
Published by LMD Publications.

Hello everyone!

I am six years old, and my name is Max,
I have a story to tell, so please sit back and relax.

I'm going to tell you all about my life,
the good, the bad, my worries and strife.
I live at home with my mum, dad, and sisters two,
one is called Jorgie, she's a little baby boo.
The other is Daisy and she's older than me,
she's nine years old and as tall as a tree.

I love my sister! I can't tell you how much I do,
but sometimes she can make me feel so very blue.
It doesn't feel nice when you love someone so much,
but you don't want to go out with them as such.
I know how this will end, it happens every time,
whenever we go out it feels like a crime.

Some places we go, people stand and stare,
some people even move away and stand over there.
When this happens, I have lots of feelings inside,
sometimes I feel embarrassed, I want to get away and hide.
But the main thing that makes me very sad,
is the fact that I know my sister, and she isn't really bad.

Things get too much for Daisy, I feel bad for her,
all of her senses change, and things become a blur.
She doesn't mean to hit, shout or scream,
all that she needs is for us to work as a team.

This might be something new for people to see,
but it's all too familiar for Mum, Dad and me.

It gets me upset to see Mummy in pain,
I want to take those bad feelings and
flush them right down the drain.

I have many feelings throughout every day,
some of them I like, others I wish them away.
Having a sister like Daisy is an emotional ride,
but I wouldn't want anyone else stood by my side.

It is normal for me to
have lots of emotion,
sometimes they mix together,
like a big witches potion.

I can be happy, excited and
want to shout out with glee,
this is what feels
very natural to me.

Emotions are like layers
and that is one of mine,
although they feel the best,
the rest I shouldn't confine.

Even though I hate the guilt and
the anger that starts brewing,
that I have towards Daisy,
because of the things she is doing.

Mummy says it's normal for me to feel this way,
and my emotions will change depending on the day.
Daisy, you see has lots of support,
but I sometimes find, I have nowhere to report.
Mummy noticed this fact and said, "that's enough!"
What we did next was extremely tough....

We went to the park! Mummy, me and baby boo,
leaving Daisy at home with Daddy, really, it's true!

We all felt bad and wondered how it would go,
I will tell you how it went, just so you all know.

If you're ever in my shoes and you feel kind of bad,
if you don't have time for yourself, you will simply go mad.
If like me, you have a super sister like Daisy,
you will know that they can often drive you crazy.

I want you to know that you aren't alone.
It's fine to speak to someone and have a little moan.
Maybe talk to someone who lives in your house,
you can even talk quietly, as if you were a mouse.
Don't keep your feelings in, if they need to come out.
If it helps you, be loud and SHOUT, SHOUT, SHOUT!

My sister has autism,
that's the superpower that she's got.
But what about me? I also must deal with a lot.
I'm an Autism Brother, and it's part of the game,
from now on I swear, I will not feel any shame.

We are all made different,
I'm sure you can see,
I am lucky that
Daisy was given to me.

So, for all you Autism Brothers,
and Sisters as well,
you are doing simply great,
so please do not dwell.

Dedication

It gives me the greatest amount of joy to dedicate this book to my three wonderfully unique amazing children - Daisy, Max and Jorgie-Rose. Also, my husband and incredible daddy to our three, Jack. You are my everything and I love you all beyond words. Thank you for believing in me and giving me the strength I needed when times got tough.

A huge thank you to Jack and Uncles Craig, Scott, Matty and Benny who completed the 'Yorkshire Three Peaks Challenge' in order to raise money towards the printing of this book. I can't tell you how much I appreciate your amazing efforts, it will hopefully mean this book can reach many more children who are struggling.

Also, a big thank you to my mum and dad for their huge donation towards the illustrations done for the book, and for everyone else who donated, without you this book wouldn't be possible.
Bec x